BUILDER OF ALL THINGS

STUDY GUIDE

Copyright © 2025 by Richie Breaux

Published by AVAIL

All rights reserved. No portion of this book may be reproduced, stored in a retrieval system, or transmitted in any form or by any means—electronic, mechanical, photocopy, recording, scanning, or other—except for brief quotations in critical reviews or articles, without prior written permission of the author.

Unless otherwise noted, all Scripture quotations are taken from the Holy Bible, New International Version®, NIV®. Copyright © 1973, 1978, 1984, 2011 by Biblica, Inc.™ Used by permission of Zondervan. All rights reserved worldwide. www.zondervan.com. The "NIV" and "New International Version" are trademarks registered in the United States Patent and Trademark Office by Biblica, Inc.™ | Scripture quotations marked ESV are from The ESV® Bible (The Holy Bible, English Standard Version®), copyright © 2001 by Crossway, a publishing ministry of Good News Publishers. Used by permission. All rights reserved. | Scripture quotations marked NLT are taken from the Holy Bible, New Living Translation, copyright © 1996, 2004, 2015 by Tyndale House Foundation. Used by permission of Tyndale House Publishers, Inc., Carol Stream, Illinois 60188. All rights reserved.

For foreign and subsidiary rights, contact the author.

Cover design & photo by Michael B. Hardie

ISBN: 978-1-964794-63-1   1 2 3 4 5 6 7 8 9 10

Printed in the United States of America

BUILDER OF ALL THINGS

STUDY GUIDE

CONTENTS

THE POWER OF SEEING CLEARLY: AUTHOR NOTE 6

INTRODUCTION. **ALL ABOARD** 8

PART 1. BUILDING TOGETHER

CHAPTER 1. **THE SKIPPER:** *Builder of All Things* 14

CHAPTER 2. **THE SHIPMATE:** *Two Boats* 20

PART 2. BEGINNING THE COURSE

CHAPTER 3. **THE STREAM:** *Heart of a King* 28

CHAPTER 4. **THE SAIL:** *The Wind Blows* 34

CHAPTER 5. **THE SWIM:** *The 153 Season* 40

PART 3. BATTLING ADVERSITY

CHAPTER 6. **THE STORM:** *Wake Him Up* 48

CHAPTER 7. **THE SNAKE:** *Air Jordan on 'Em* 54

CHAPTER 8. **THE SMOKE:** *Self-Inflicted Wounds* 60

PART 4. BIRTHING THE LEGACY

CHAPTER 9. **THE SUN:** *All Things New* 68

CHAPTER 10. **THE SCORE:** *We Already Won* 74

BUILDER OF ALL THINGS

A NEW
PERSPECTIVE OF PURPOSE
WITH THE
'BUSINESS PARTNER'
YOU DIDN'T KNOW
YOU HAD

RICHIE BREAUX

THE POWER OF SEEING CLEARLY:
Author Note

Before anything can be built, something has to be seen. This means we've got to survey the land—look at the existing conditions, the blueprints, and the design. We don't break ground until we've taken in what's already there.

If any of us are going to partner with God as the Builder of All Things, the first thing we've got to do is pause and pay attention. That starts by asking simple but hard questions:

- What do I believe?
- Why do I think this way?
- What lens am I reading life through?

When we slow down long enough to answer those questions, something powerful happens. We pull our thoughts off autopilot. We stop coasting and start seeing.

Most of us interpret God, people, pain, and purpose through a filter we didn't even know was there, and until we name that filter, we'll keep reading truth like it's bad news or miss it altogether.

This process is like holding up a mirror—not directly to our face, but to our mindset. We might begin to notice patterns:

"I expect disappointment."
"I assume people are against me."
"I hear grace but still feel like I have to earn everything."

That's perception. That's our lens. And we can't clean a lens we won't admit is dirty. This is why reflection matters. Honest self-inventory exposes what doesn't line up with the truth.

Sometimes, it's not the smoke we're stuck in; it's a lie we've believed for years. Hurt, fear, shame, bad teaching . . . all of it becomes a lens. But when we see it, we can bring it to the light. That's how change begins, with clarity. My invitation:

What you see matters, but how do you respond to what you see?

That's everything. Clarity is a gift, but it's what you do with it that changes your life. If you don't like what you see, I encourage you to change it. But don't look away; face it. Call it what it is. You can't change what you're still excusing. Breakthrough starts with honesty. Healing begins when truth steps into the room. You're not stuck. You're being invited to see it differently so you can live differently. Let's build from there.

INTRODUCTION

ALL ABOARD

> *"I believe each of us has something important to steward."*

READING TIME

As you read the Introduction: "All Aboard" in *Builder of All Things*, review, reflect on, and respond to the text by answering the following questions.

REFLECT AND TAKE ACTION:

What specific burdens are you carrying right now that you've convinced yourself are yours alone?

_____
_____
_____
_____
_____
_____
_____
_____

Think back to a time when you achieved a goal, only to find yourself immediately reaching for the next one. Did that victory satisfy you, or did it just change the size of your problems? What does this reveal about your definition of success?

_____
_____
_____
_____
_____
_____
_____
_____

Have you ever found yourself searching for external answers when, deep down, you already knew what you needed to do? What stopped you from taking action?

_____
_____
_____
_____
_____
_____
_____
_____

If you were to fully lean on God for wisdom and direction, what major decision would you make differently starting today?

_____
_____
_____
_____
_____
_____
_____
_____

What does good stewardship look like for you right now? In what ways do you find yourself stewarding your calling well, and in what ways could you steward it better?

_____
_____
_____
_____

What do you hope to gain from this study guide, and how will you intentionally apply its insights to create real change in your life?

PART 1

BUILDING TOGETHER

CHAPTER 1

THE SKIPPER:
Builder of All Things

"Like a muscle, faith can get stronger and stronger, or it can potentially get injured if we are not in the presence of a spotter."

READING TIME

As you read Chapter 1: "THE SKIPPER: Builder of All Things" in *Builder of All Things*, reflect on, and respond to the text by answering the following questions.

REFLECT AND TAKE ACTION:

Think about a time in your life when a shift in perspective dramatically changed the way you viewed a situation. How did that shift impact your actions and decisions?

_____
_____
_____
_____
_____
_____
_____
_____

Have you ever had a moment when you realized how small your struggles were in comparison to God's bigger picture? How did it affect your approach to leadership and problem-solving?

_____
_____
_____
_____
_____
_____
_____
_____

> *"For every house is built by someone, but the builder of all things is God."*
> **—Hebrews 3:4 (ESV)**

Consider the scripture above and answer the following questions:

What does it mean to recognize God as the ultimate Builder in your personal and professional life? Are you allowing God to take His rightful place as your Builder? Why or why not?

_____
_____
_____
_____
_____
_____

How does this verse challenge the way you see your role as a leader, business owner, or ministry worker?

_____
_____
_____
_____
_____
_____

Have you ever been in a situation where you had to step out in faith without clear direction? What happened?

_____
_____
_____

Where in your life or leadership are you letting fear hold you back?

Who in your life has played the role of a "spotter" for you, and how has their support helped you stay on course?

How has isolation impacted your ability to lead and persevere in the past? To what extent does isolation impact you now, and what can you do to ensure you're surrounded by the right "spotters"?

_____
_____
_____
_____
_____

What areas of your leadership or personal life are you still holding onto as if they belong to you rather than seeing them as something entrusted to you by God?

_____
_____
_____
_____
_____

How do you seek and discern God's guidance when making difficult decisions? Provide an example of how you have done this in your own business.

_____
_____
_____
_____
_____

Have you ever felt a deep burden for a problem that led you into a new calling or direction? How did you respond to that burden?

_____
_____
_____
_____

In what ways do you see God shaping you, much like a builder carefully constructs a house? What areas of your life are still "under construction"?

_____
_____
_____
_____

What resonated with you in the chapter's song pairing, "Background"? How does its message connect to your calling, business, or relationship with God? What steps can you take to integrate that lesson into your work?

_____
_____
_____
_____

CHAPTER 2

THE SHIPMATE:
Two Boats

"Sometimes, the breakthrough you're looking for comes when you're humble enough to listen to the people around you."

READING TIME

As you read Chapter 2: "THE SHIPMATE: Two Boats" in Builder of All Things, reflect on, and respond to the text by answering the following questions.

REFLECT AND TAKE ACTION:

Have you ever been in a situation where you felt like giving up but sensed God urging you to keep going? What was the result of pushing through?

_____
_____
_____
_____
_____
_____
_____
_____
_____

How do you personally recognize when you are in a season of "washing the nets" in your life or leadership?

_____
_____
_____
_____
_____
_____
_____
_____
_____

"We've worked hard all night and haven't caught anything."
—Luke 5:5 (ESV)

Consider the scripture above and answer the following questions:

Peter was exhausted but obeyed Jesus when He told him to cast the nets one more time. Have you ever experienced a moment when you obeyed God despite fatigue or doubt? What about a time when you *didn't* obey? What happened in each scenario?

_____

_____

_____

_____

_____

_____

What does this verse teach us about faith, perseverance, and trusting in God's timing?

_____

_____

_____

_____

_____

_____

What areas of your life or leadership might be cluttered with self-reliance, preventing you from fully letting Jesus in?

_____

_____

_____

Who in your life acts as your shipmate, helping you carry the weight of leadership, faith, or personal growth? How have they impacted your journey?

Can you recall a time when pride kept you from the right path? What about a time when humility allowed you to receive advice that changed your direction? What did you learn?

Who in your business complements your strengths and can strengthen and refine your vision? Who in your business seems to be misaligned with your vision, and what needs to happen to secure that alignment?

_____
_____
_____
_____
_____
_____
_____

In what areas of your life have you seen God provide in ways that exceeded your expectations?

_____
_____
_____
_____
_____
_____

Have you ever resisted stepping back from something because of fear? What might God be asking you to release or reassess right now?

_____
_____

How has God used people in your life to carry the burden of business ownership? Have you ever had someone unexpectedly show up just when you needed help?

What resonated with you in the chapter's song pairing, "All I Need Is You"? How does its message connect to your calling, business, or relationship with God? What steps can you take to integrate that lesson into your work?

PART 2

BEGINNING THE COURSE

CHAPTER 3

THE STREAM:
Heart of a King

> *"Seeing God as the true owner of your company lifts that heavy weight off your shoulders."*

READING TIME

As you read Chapter 3: "THE STREAM: Heart of a King" in *Builder of All Things*, reflect on, and respond to the text by answering the following questions.

REFLECT AND TAKE ACTION:

Have you ever been so focused on the work in front of you that you lost sight of your bigger purpose? What did it take to regain clarity?

_____
_____
_____
_____
_____
_____
_____
_____
_____

Have you ever felt like you were drifting without a clear destination? What steps can you take to let God establish your course?

_____
_____
_____
_____
_____
_____
_____
_____
_____

> "The king's heart is a stream of water directed by the LORD; he guides it wherever he pleases."
> **—Proverbs 21:1 (NLT)**

Consider the scripture above and answer the following questions:

How does knowing that God directs even the hearts of leaders challenge the way you approach your own leadership or business? What does it mean to you for God to direct your heart, and in what ways have you experienced that?

_____

_____

_____

_____

_____

What is your first reaction to the idea that your business is in God's hands and that He is the owner?

_____

_____

_____

_____

_____

What personal ambitions might be distracting you from God's greater vision for your life?

_____

_____

How often do you allow fear to dictate your decisions? Provide an example. What can you do differently next time?

In this chapter, the ocean (vast, aimless drifting) is contrasted with the stream (a clear path set by God). Which metaphor best describes your life and leadership right now, and why?

How do you define success? Does your definition align with God's?

_____
_____
_____
_____
_____
_____

Can you identify a past disappointment that later turned out to be a necessary redirection? What did you learn from it?

_____
_____
_____
_____
_____
_____

What does your current balance between work, relationships, and faith look like? What needs to change?

_____
_____
_____

_____
_____
_____

What does it mean for you to truly see yourself as a steward rather than the owner of your business, ministry, or leadership role? How would your business look different with this lens?

_____
_____
_____
_____
_____

What resonated with you in the chapter's song pairing, "Journey"? How does its message connect to your calling, business, or relationship with God? What steps can you take to integrate that lesson into your work?

_____
_____
_____
_____
_____

CHAPTER 4

THE SAIL:
The Wind Blows

"There will come moments in life when we have to make a choice to step through the door with faith or stay where it feels safe."

READING TIME

As you read Chapter 4: "THE SAIL: The Wind Blows" in Builder of All Things, reflect on, and respond to the text by answering the following questions.

REFLECT AND TAKE ACTION:

Think of a time when you faced a pivotal decision. Did you step through the door, or did you hesitate? What happened as a result?

_____
_____
_____
_____
_____
_____
_____
_____
_____

When was the last time you felt an internal nudge to do something bold? Did you follow it? Why or why not?

_____
_____
_____
_____
_____
_____
_____
_____
_____
_____

> *"I will instruct you and teach you in the way you should go; I will counsel you with my loving eye on you."*
> **—Psalm 32:8**

Consider the scripture above and answer the following questions:

Reflect on a time when you sensed His instruction or counsel directing your path in business. How has that experience shaped your ability to surrender to His direction in your decisions today?

_____

_____

_____

_____

_____

What is one recent decision where you prioritized your own reasoning over seeking God's wisdom? How did that choice impact you and those around you?

_____

_____

_____

_____

_____

What is one moment in your life where you felt like you were just "drifting," but later saw God's hand at work?

_____

_____

What past season of your life—one that may have seemed disconnected or even wasted—do you now realize was training ground for where you are today?

What is one area of your life where you need to be more aware of God's movement? How will you commit to listening more intentionally?

Who in your life has seen the potential in you before you saw it in yourself? Who in your life are you meant to encourage, mentor, or out greatness in? What is one practical way you can do that this week?

_____
_____
_____
_____
_____
_____
_____

Looking back on the past five years, what are three unexpected ways God has led you that you wouldn't have chosen for yourself? How did those moments prepare you for where you are today?

_____
_____
_____
_____
_____
_____
_____

In times of uncertainty, it's easy to doubt our path. What is one thing you absolutely know to be true about your calling, even when everything else feels unclear?

_____
_____
_____
_____
_____
_____
_____
_____

What resonated with you in the chapter's song pairing, "I'll Find You"? How does its message connect to your calling, business, or relationship with God? What steps can you take to integrate that lesson into your work?

_____
_____
_____
_____
_____
_____
_____
_____

CHAPTER 5

THE SWIM:
The 153 Season

"Faith without action is dead, but action without faith misses the whole point."

READING TIME

As you read Chapter 5: "THE SWIM: The 153 Season" in Builder of All Things, reflect on, and respond to the text by answering the following questions.

REFLECT AND TAKE ACTION:

Have you ever worked tirelessly at something only to realize later that it was God who made the breakthrough happen? What did you learn from that experience?

_____
_____
_____
_____
_____
_____
_____
_____
_____

Are there areas in your life where you've been waiting for results but haven't taken action to prepare? What's one step you can take today to act in faith?

_____
_____
_____
_____
_____
_____
_____
_____
_____

> *"Throw your net on the right side of the boat and you will find some."*
> **—John 21:6**

Consider the scripture above and answer the following questions:

The disciples had spent the whole night fishing with no results, but when Jesus told them where to cast their nets, they pulled in a massive catch. Have you ever felt like you were doing everything right but still coming up empty? How do you discern whether you need to persist or shift directions?

_____

_____

_____

_____

Can you think of a time when you followed God's prompting, even when it seemed illogical? What was the outcome?

_____

_____

_____

_____

Have you faced a situation where what seemed like a major setback turned into a season of new opportunities? What changed in your mindset or approach?

_____

_____

_____

What's an area of your life where you've been hesitating to act? What would it look like to respond with the same urgency and trust Peter had?

How can you recognize when you're entering a "153 season"? What practical steps can you take to ensure you're ready when the opportunity arrives?

Where in your life do you need to surrender your approach and be open to a new way of doing things?

_____
_____
_____
_____
_____
_____

What is one area of your life where you currently see God's intentionality at work? How is it impacting the way you approach your business?

_____
_____
_____
_____
_____
_____

Have you ever faced a situation where taking a shortcut seemed appealing? Did you take it, and if so, what would have happened if you had chosen not to take it?

_____
_____

What's something you've been doing out of routine or habit rather than true faith and expectation? What would it look like to shift your mindset to bring faith into your actions?

What resonated with you in the chapter's song pairing, "Celebrate More"? How does its message connect to your calling, business, or relationship with God? What steps can you take to integrate that lesson into your work?

PART 3

BATTLING ADVERSITY

CHAPTER 6

THE STORM:
Wake Him Up

> *"When you anchor yourself to the One who builds it all, the storm doesn't own you."*

READING TIME

As you read Chapter 6: "THE STORM: Wake Him Up" in Builder of All Things, reflect on, and respond to the text by answering the following questions.

REFLECT AND TAKE ACTION:

Think of a time when you saw the signs of an impending "storm" in your life but ignored them. What were the warning signs, and what would you have done differently?

_____
_____
_____
_____
_____
_____
_____
_____

The disciples panicked in the boat while Jesus slept. Have you ever faced a crisis where it felt like God was silent? How did you respond, and looking back, what do you think He was trying to teach you?

_____
_____
_____
_____
_____
_____
_____

> *"Suddenly a furious storm came up on the lake, so that the waves swept over the boat. But Jesus was sleeping. The disciples went and woke him, saying, 'Lord, save us! We're going to drown!'" He replied, "You of little faith, why are you so afraid?" Then he got up and rebuked the wind and waves, and it was completely calm."*
> **—Matthew 8:24-26**

Consider the scripture above and answer the following questions:

The disciples cried out in fear, but Jesus rebuked their lack of faith. When you're in a storm, do you operate more out of fear or faith? What practical steps can you take to shift toward faith in those moments?

_____
_____
_____
_____
_____
_____
_____

The disciples saw Jesus's power over the storm and asked, "Who is this?" When has God shown up in a way that left you in awe? How did it change your faith?

_____
_____
_____
_____
_____
_____
_____

Think of a time when you had to lead others through a crisis. How did your response impact the outcome?

_____
_____
_____
_____
_____
_____

What's one difficult season in your life that ultimately strengthened you? How did it prepare you for what came next?

_____
_____
_____
_____
_____
_____

Have you ever experienced a season where everything seemed to fall apart, only to later realize it was positioning you for something greater? What was that moment?

_____
_____
_____
_____
_____

Reflect on a storm you are currently facing in your life or business. In what area of your life do you need to stop trying to handle everything yourself and instead invite God into the situation?

_____
_____
_____
_____
_____

In the *Titanic* analogy, Rose asks the architect for the truth about the ship. When facing difficulties, do you seek out hard truths, or do you avoid them? Why is it important to have the courage to face reality in leadership?

_____
_____
_____
_____
_____

Have you ever experienced a forced redirection that, though painful, ultimately led to a better path? How can you reframe current challenges in light of God's sovereignty?

_____
_____
_____
_____
_____

When everything else is shaken, what core truths do you hold onto that keep you steady? How can you strengthen that foundation now, before the next storm comes?

_____
_____
_____
_____
_____

What resonated with you in the chapter's song pairing, "Drown"? How does its message connect to your calling, business, or relationship with God? What steps can you take to integrate that lesson into your work?

_____
_____
_____
_____
_____

CHAPTER 7

THE SNAKE:
Air Jordan on 'Em

"Don't fight the snake on its terms."

READING TIME

As you read Chapter 7: "THE SNAKE: Air Jordan on 'Em" in *Builder of All Things*, reflect on, and respond to the text by answering the following questions.

REFLECT AND TAKE ACTION:

How do you discern the difference between a storm and a snake?

_____
_____
_____
_____
_____
_____
_____
_____
_____

Think of a time when you fell for the bait—whether it was responding emotionally to a situation, falling into fear, or allowing negativity to dictate your choices. What would you do differently now?

_____
_____
_____
_____
_____
_____
_____
_____

> *"Now the serpent was more crafty than any of the wild animals the Lord God had made. He said to the woman, 'Did God really say, "You must not eat from any tree in the garden"?'"*
> **—Genesis 3:1**

Consider the scripture above and answer the following questions:

How do subtle doubts or misleading narratives in your business or leadership mirror the serpent's question in Genesis 3:1 ("Did God really say . . . ?")? How are you recognizing and responding to these deceptive narratives?

_____
_____
_____
_____
_____
_____

What seeds of doubt is the snake planting, and in what ways are they affecting your business?

_____
_____
_____
_____
_____

Consider the three questions posed in this chapter about taking the bait, and take some time to answer each of them:

1. Is the bait challenging the truth with lies?

_____
_____

2. Is it pushing you toward unhealthy reliance?

3. Is it undermining your core beliefs and values?

Have you ever had a situation where your vulnerabilities were targeted, like the enemy was trying to discredit or discourage you? How did you handle it?

What is one area of your life in which you need to resist the urge to fight in the mud and instead take the battle higher?

_____
_____
_____
_____

Have you ever faced a situation where shifting to gratitude changed the outcome or your attitude? What specific aspects of your life or business are you thankful for today, and how have they impacted your journey?

_____
_____
_____
_____

Consider the three questions posed in this chapter about taking the bait, and take some time to answer each of them:

   1. Are you justifying things that harm you?

_____
_____
_____
_____

   2. Are your weaknesses being exploited?

_____
_____

_____

_____

3. Are you questioning your purpose or worth?

_____

_____

_____

_____

Think of a recent conflict, either in your business or personal life. Did you fight in the mud, or did you elevate? What was the result?

_____

_____

_____

_____

_____

What resonated with you in the chapter's song pairing, "Set Me Free"? How does its message connect to your calling, business, or relationship with God? What steps can you take to integrate that lesson into your work?

_____

_____

_____

_____

_____

CHAPTER 8

THE SMOKE:
Self-Inflicted Wounds

"Fires happen. Smoke will appear. The question isn't whether you'll face these challenges; it's what you'll do when you see the first sign of smoke."

READING TIME

As you read Chapter 8: "THE SMOKE: Self-Inflicted Wounds" in Builder of All Things, reflect on, and respond to the text by answering the following questions.

REFLECT AND TAKE ACTION:

"The smoke" is self-inflicted—often caused by ego, emotional residue, or misplaced effort. Have you ever made a decision based on one of these factors that later led to regret? What was the outcome, and what did you learn?

_____
_____
_____
_____
_____
_____
_____

What is currently clouding your judgment, and what steps can you take to clear the air before making your next major decision?

_____
_____
_____
_____
_____
_____
_____

> *"Whoever digs a pit will fall into it."*
> **—Proverbs 26:27**

Consider the scripture above and answer the following questions:

The verse warns that the harm we set in motion can eventually trap us. Have you ever experienced a situation where a small compromise led to larger unintended consequences? How did you recover?

_____
_____
_____
_____
_____
_____

What guardrails can you put in place to prevent yourself from "digging a pit" that could ultimately backfire?

_____
_____
_____
_____
_____
_____

Can you think of a moment when your ego led you down the wrong path? What did it cost you, and how can you avoid repeating that mistake?

_____
_____

Can you identify a past "flash point" in your business, leadership, or personal life? What warning signs did you ignore before it became a bigger problem?

Is there unresolved frustration, resentment, or fear in your life that may be affecting your leadership or relationships? What do you need to do to release it?

What's one truth about yourself or your leadership that you've been avoiding because it's uncomfortable? What would it look like to face it head-on?

_____
_____
_____
_____
_____
_____
_____

What is one area in your leadership or business where you've been avoiding taking action? What is at stake if you continue to ignore it?

_____
_____
_____
_____
_____
_____
_____

How has a past crisis reshaped your priorities? What did you learn about yourself through that experience?

_____
_____

What proactive steps can you take today to fireproof your business, relationships, or personal integrity from future crises?

What resonated with you in the chapter's song pairing, "Deconstruction"? How does its message connect to your calling, business, or relationship with God? What steps can you take to integrate that lesson into your work?

PART 4

BIRTHING THE LEGACY

CHAPTER 9

THE SUN:
All Things New

> *"Without Him, the bricks and mortar of your success will crumble under the weight of their own emptiness."*

READING TIME

As you read Chapter 9: "THE SUN: All Things New" in *Builder of All Things*, reflect on, and respond to the text by answering the following questions.

REFLECT AND TAKE ACTION:

Think of a time when you came through a difficult season—how did the "sunrise" look for you? What did you gain from the process?

_____
_____
_____
_____
_____
_____
_____
_____

What are you reaching toward for strength? Is it truly sustaining you, or is it temporary?

_____
_____
_____
_____
_____
_____
_____
_____
_____
_____
_____

> *"Weeping may last through the night, but joy comes with the morning."*
> **—Psalms 30:5 (NLT)**

Consider the scripture above and answer the following questions:

Have you ever faced a loss or disappointment that made joy seem impossible? How did you eventually find healing?

_____
_____
_____
_____
_____
_____

How does this verse challenge you to change your perspective on hardship, knowing that joy is coming even when it doesn't feel like it?

_____
_____
_____
_____
_____
_____

What painful experience has reshaped how you approach life, relationships, or leadership?

_____
_____
_____

Where in your life do you need to shift from focusing on what's missing to appreciating what's still present?

What are the "light sources" in your life that keep you energized, and are they leading you toward lasting growth or temporary satisfaction?

What's one habit you can implement today to practice presence and gratitude?

_____
_____
_____
_____
_____

How often do you rush through life, missing the beauty in the process? What can you do to slow down and appreciate where you are right now?

_____
_____
_____
_____
_____
_____

Have you been building any part of your life—business, relationships, identity—on shaky ground? What would it take to rebuild it on something solid?

_____
_____
_____

Do you find yourself constantly looking for the "next big thing"? In what ways can your current circumstances serve as a source of contentment in your life?

What resonated with you in the chapter's song pairing, "8:28"? How does its message connect to your calling, business, or relationship with God? What steps can you take to integrate that lesson into your work?

CHAPTER 10

THE SCORE:
We Already Won

"The perspective you choose to adopt can keep you stagnant and chained or it can set you free."

READING TIME

As you read Chapter 10: "THE SCORE: We Already Won" in *Builder of All Things*, reflect on, and respond to the text by answering the following questions.

REFLECT AND TAKE ACTION:

Consider a setback or challenge you are currently facing. If you knew the ultimate victory was already secured, what specific fear, habit, or mindset would you release today? Why haven't you let go of it yet?

_____
_____
_____
_____
_____
_____
_____
_____
_____

Imagine watching the hardest moment of your life on replay. How did you win in the end, and how would you have handled that moment differently?

_____
_____
_____
_____
_____
_____
_____
_____
_____

> *"For I can do everything through Christ, who gives me strength."*
> **—Philippians 4:13 (NLT)**

Consider the scripture above and answer the following questions:

Paul wrote this verse while in prison, yet he still believed he had strength through Christ. If you had nothing left—no success, no reputation, no security—would you still believe that Christ is enough? Why or why not?

_____
_____
_____
_____
_____

What difficult reality are you currently facing that requires the same level of unshakeable trust that Paul had in this verse?

_____
_____
_____
_____
_____

What is the one lie about yourself that has held you captive for years? What truth can you hold onto to replace that lie?

_____
_____

What is the "small chain" in your life—something insignificant—that you've allowed to control you for too long?

If today was your last day, would you be content with the legacy you've built? What would you regret not doing, saying, or changing?

If you had just one year left to live, who would you forgive, what relationships would you mend, and what risks would you finally take? Why are you waiting?

_____
_____
_____
_____
_____
_____
_____

When you imagine the end of your life, what do you desperately hope people will say about you? Are you living in a way that ensures they will?

_____
_____
_____
_____
_____
_____

Where in your life are you relying on your own strength instead of trusting Jesus? How is that working out for you?

_____
_____
_____

_____

_____

_____

What is the one thing you've been too afraid to do because of what people might think? What would it look like to stop caring and finally step into it?

_____

_____

_____

_____

_____

_____

What resonated with you in the chapter's song pairing, "I Still Believe"? How does its message connect to your calling, business, or relationship with God? What steps can you take to integrate that lesson into your work?

_____

_____

_____

_____

_____

_____

www.ingramcontent.com/pod-product-compliance
Lightning Source LLC
Chambersburg PA
CBHW062120080426
42734CB00012B/2929